Yeah right.

Tui

Yeah right.

Hodder Moa

A catalogue record for this book is available from the National Library of New Zealand.

A Hodder Moa Book
First published in 2005 by Hachette Livre NZ Ltd
4 Whetu Place, Mairangi Bay
Auckland, New Zealand

Reprinted 2005, 2006 (twice)

ISBN-10: 1-86971-046-0
ISBN-13: 978-1-86971-046-0

Designed and produced by Hachette Livre NZ Ltd
Printed by Everbest Printing Co. Ltd, China

To the public of New Zealand for being able to laugh at yourselves, and for providing a constant supply of rich and humorous material.

Introduction

New Zealanders are a serious lot, who dislike fun and are totally devoid of humour — yeah right! Actually, we have a unique outlook — we know 'she'll be right', we don't take life too seriously and while we will laugh at others, we are also just as happy to laugh at ourselves. This inherent knack to see the funny side has given Tui the opportunity to lighten up everyone's day.

Tui has taken a unique piece of Kiwi vernacular and developed it into a distinctive social commentary. From politics to rugby, from banter between mates at the pub to flatmates' financial woes, from TV programming to things that are just fundamentally wrong, the **Yeah right** billboards have always reflected New Zealand life and society.

Lots of fun has been had in creating and executing the **Yeah right** campaign. The billboard fodder has not only come from the wits at Tui. We have had great suggestions from numerous sources, such as competitions in bars, the Tui website, TV programmes and from those who love the campaign — you, our drinkers (and those of you yet to be converted!).

Such has been their impact that the **Yeah right** billboards have often been 'hijacked' to help promote an individual's opinion in a desperate attempt to be noticed. Some quick-witted punter even changed the '*I slept on my mate's couch* — **Yeah right**' to '*I slept on my mate, ouch'.* Factions and groups, too, have used the billboards to make their viewpoints known about issues such as policing numbers, fishing rights, the Iraq war or the Civil Union Bill.

To compile this book, we have spent years observing the subtlety and nuances of the intricacies of New Zealanders' quirky habits, demeanor and verbal exchanges. We hope that you enjoy this selection, collated from an array of **Yeah right** billboards dating back to 1997.

We hope that New Zealand will continue to provide a delightful, rich supply of raw material for Tui to comment on and, if that upsets one or two people along the way . . . well, no offence intended.

Little Johnny
Halfback, social commentator and Tui drinker

**Let your mum stay
as long as she likes.**

We spent the whole weekend fishing.

Yeah right.

Tui

I think we should take things slowly.

I stayed at a mate's place.

I wouldn't say it if I didn't mean it.

Yeah right.

Tui

Someone else used my credit card.

Yeah right.

Tui

Trim the sides, but leave it long at the back — ta.

Yeah right.

Tui

I only read it for the articles.

Yeah right.

Tui

**Moving in together
is a great idea.**

**It's just what
I always wanted.**

Yeah right.

Tui

Free latte bowl with every dozen Tui sold.

It's getting too
cold for a beer.

Yeah right.

Tui

I'll get in with jeans and jandals.

Yeah right.

Tui

Beer doesn't really go with that.

Yeah right.

Tui

For sale: Holden HQ, peach with lavender trim.

Quiet student seeks room.

The flat looks perfect, here's your bond back.

Yeah right.

Tui

Kiwi Bank? I'd trust the government with my money.

Yeah right.

Tui

Hey Augie — what's the weather going to do?

Yeah right.

Tui

Enthusiastic, but often 'wide of the mark', former TV3 weather man, Augie Auer.

You know the odds, now beat them.

Carols by candlelight.

Yeah right.

Tui

Let's scrap the NPC.

Yeah right.

Tui

It's only done 40,000kms. Yeah right.

There are no skeletons in Rodney's closet.

Yeah right.

Aimed at parliament's most vocal perk-buster.

The perfect body in just 3 minutes a day.

Yeah right.

Tui

With petrol prices this high, I'm giving up beer.

Yeah right.

Tui

I can give up anytime.

Yeah right.

Tui

I'm fine — I've just got something in my eye.

Yeah right.

Tui

Can't wait for those Xmas cracker jokes.

Yeah right.

Tui

Field Days is all about business.

Yeah right.

Tui

The bridge should be clear now.

On the Auckland motorway, leading up to the infamous traffic bottleneck.

I was unaware of the staff dating policy.

Yeah right.

Tui

Only if my girlfriend lets me.

Put the ham in the beer fridge.

Yeah right.

Tui

It's a Swedish
documentary.

Yeah right.

Tui

I was reading her t-shirt.

Yeah right.

Tui

**Guys look great
in Speedos.**

Those websites are work-related.

Yeah right.

Tui

I'll just watch the first half.

I'll come straight home after the game.

Yeah right.

Tui

Make mine a shandy.

Yeah right.

Tui

**The flat account
will cover it.**

Yeah right.

Tui

It actually makes your bum look smaller.

**Not all guys
think like that.**

I hardly noticed her moustache.

Yeah right.

Tui

Weddings are more than just free beer.

Of course I remember your name.

I'm really keen to see your mother again.

Yeah right.

Tui

It's true, a guy at the pub told me.

Yeah right.

Tui

It's better to give
than receive.

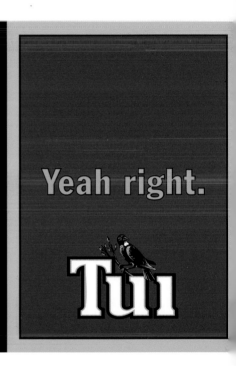

I've been training all summer.

Yeah right.

Tui

I've worn that heaps since you gave it to me.

It was a legitimate business expense.

assive lunch claims by TVNZ senior executives.

Just popping out for a 4km swim, 180km bike and 42km run.

Yeah right.

Tui

She doesn't believe in Valentine's Day.

Save power, turn off the beer fridge.

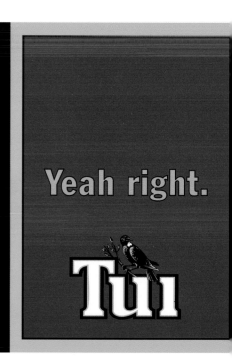

I'll get a Brazilian if you do.

**We shouldn't,
we're flatmates.**

Yeah right.

Tui

We'll play your CDs later on.

**Lots of people take
6 years to graduate.**

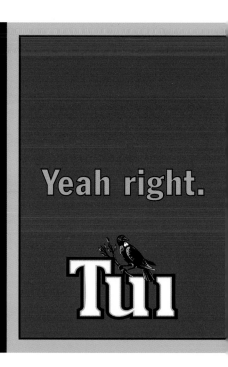

I only had a massage.

Yeah right.

Tui

It's not about winning, it's about participating.

Yeah right.

Tui

You look great in flannel PJs.

What goes on tour, stays on tour.

I hope it doesn't turn into a catfight.

Yes, I've read the instructions.

Yeah right.

Tui

They're real.

Yeah right.

Tui

I'm not drinking 'til after exams.

Yeah right.

Tui

Here, you have the tongs.

Yeah right.

Tui

See you at Revival on Sunday.

Yeah right.

Tui

In response to the Revival Church in Taranaki, who created their own *Yeah right* billboard, targeting beer drinkers

We wish you the best of luck.

Welcoming the 2005 Lions rugby team to New Zealand.

Her butt walked into my hand.

Yeah right.

Tui

In only 48
easy instalments.

Yeah right.

Tui

**Bikinis shouldn't
be so small.**

Yeah right.

Tui

**It's not receding,
I cut it this way.**

This year we won't offend anyone.

Yeah right.

Tui

Here. Take the beach.

Yeah right.

Tui

I don't mind paying for Auckland's roads.

We should bring
the girls next year.

Yeah right.

Tui

Please let the bus go first.

Yeah right.

Tui

**Put the power
bill in my name.**

Yeah right.

Tui

US Intelligence.

Yeah right.

Tui

**Put the motorway
in my backyard.**

After England won the 2003 Rugby Word Cup (no, we weren't bitter).

But I bought the first round.

Yeah right.

Tui

Coarse language and nudity may offend.

Come back Russell, all is forgiven.

essage to Russell Coutts after he parted company with the Alinghi syndicate in 2004.

Please hold. You're in a priority queue.

Yeah right.

Tui

...om the off-the-wall reality television show about a transsexual who misleads guys vying for her attention. ...his billboard was removed after a complaint was upheld by the Advertising Standards Complaints Board.

It's a church, not a cult.

One careful lady owner.

Yeah right.

Tui

The video store gave
me the wrong video.

Yeah right.

Tui

Make mine a salad combo. Yeah right.

Tui

Let Paul fly us there.

Yeah right.

Tui

After Paul Holmes' plane crashed — for a second time.

**Of course it's true,
I saw it on CNN.**

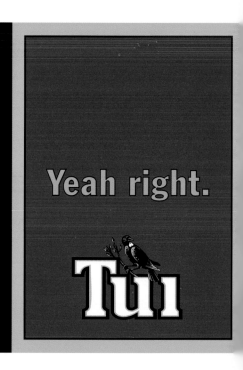

I past NCEA Inglish.

Yeah right.

Tui

Who's that
John Farnham guy?

imed at the Prime Minister for not knowing one of Australia's most famous singers.

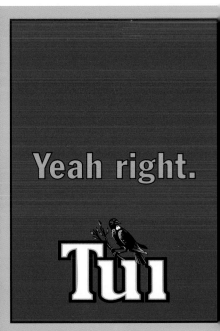

I won't pee in your wetsuit. Yeah right.

Tui

Let's go to Auckland for the holidays.

**Flight departs 11.50pm
December 31st 1999.**

Mission Estate Concert – BYO Beer Only.

**Three Wise Men,
a Virgin and a Donkey.**

Yeah right.

Tui

The cheque is in the mail.

Yeah right.

Tui

Have I got a deal for you.

Poor John Hawkesby.

ay out of squillions for TVNZ news reader after just a short time in the job.

Maybe we could have won the 2003 World Cup if the public's favourite had been there.

We will miss the Cheeky Whitey.

Paul Holmes again — this time upon his departure from TVNZ to Prime.

**They won't find me
in this hidey hole.**

Saddam Hussein thought the Americans would never find him in a global game of hide and seek.

Camilla for Queen.

Yeah right.

Tui

**They are all
worthy candidates.**

Aren't local body elections a fun and exciting time for us all?

Hasn't Dick made a difference?

Yeah right.

Tui

x months after Dick Hubbard was elected Auckland Mayor (hope he proves us wrong).

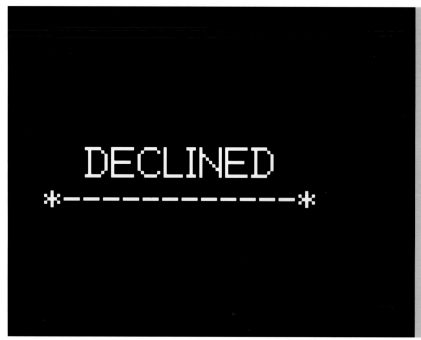